Kingston Libraries

This item can be returned

o'

Royal
Kingst

GUINEA PIGS

Dennis Kelsey-Wood

GUINEA PIG PRIMER
Common Name: guinea pig, or cavy
Scientific Name: *Cavia porcellus*
Family: Caviidae
Distribution: South America
Number of Breeds: 11—plus many
colors and patterns
Weight (Average): 2 lbs. (1,000g)
Longevity: 4 to 6 years
(maximum about 8 years)
Diet: Herbivorous
Breeding Age: Boars, 5 to 6
months; sows, 3 months
Number of Teats: 2
Number of Digits: 4 on the front feet;
3 on the rear feet
Gestation Period (Average): 68 days
Litter Size: 2 to 4 average
Condition of Young At Birth:
Fully developed,
eyes open and able to
run around within minutes
Weaning Age: 4 weeks average
Important Vitamins: Vitamin C
Preferred Temp: 63-72°F

© **T.F.H. Publications, Inc.**

Distributed in the UNITED STATES to the Pet Trade by T.F.H. Publications, Inc., 1 TFH Plaza, Neptune City, NJ 07753; on the Internet at www.tfh.com; in CANADA by Rolf C. Hagen Inc., 3225 Sartelon St., Montreal, Quebec H4R 1E8; Pet Trade by H & L Pet Supplies Inc., 27 Kingston Crescent, Kitchener, Ontario N2B 2T6; in ENGLAND by T.F.H. Publications, PO Box 74, Havant PO9 5TT; in AUSTRALIA AND THE SOUTH PACIFIC by T.F.H. (Australia), Pty. Ltd., Box 149, Brookvale 2100 N.S.W., Australia; in NEW ZEALAND by Brooklands Aquarium Ltd., 5 McGiven Drive, New Plymouth, RD1 New Zealand; in SOUTH AFRICA by Rolf C. Hagen S.A. (PTY.) LTD., P.O. Box 201199, Durban North 4016, South Africa; in JAPAN by T.F.H. Publications. Published by T.F.H. Publications, Inc.
MANUFACTURED IN THE
UNITED STATES OF AMERICA
BY T.F.H. PUBLICATIONS, INC.

CONTENTS

INTRODUCTION

The guinea pig, or cavy, was one of the first pets kept by us humans. Its path of domestication goes back about 3,000 years to the natives of South America. These peoples raised guinea pigs as a source of food—much as Europeans did with rabbits. No doubt many were also kept as hut pets. During the period of the Inca Empire, guinea pigs were selectively bred. New color forms were created, and even strains having their own flavor!

One effect of the Spanish conquest of the Incas during the 16th century was that it brought to an end the selective breeding process. Although the Conquistadors sent various color varieties of guinea pig back to Spain, structured breeding programs probably did not resume until the 19th century. This was a period of great interest in developing breeds and color variants in all mammals that have since become highly popular—from farm livestock to pets.

WHAT'S IN A NAME?

The origin of the name *guinea pig* is obscure, but a few theories have been put forward. It is said that when these little rodents first started to arrive in Britain during the 18th century, they were thought to have come from Guinea in West Africa.

It is possible that they arrived from Guiana into northern South America. The British were less familiar with this region than that of Africa, so confusion is easily appreciated. Another suggestion is that they exchanged hands for one guinea—a princely sum in those days, having a value of one pound and one shilling.

The term *pig* no doubt arose from the fact that these little animals run somewhat like pigs, bear a superficial resemblance to them, and squeal when frightened. Further, the scientific name of

A guinea pig can be a good pet for a child, provided that the youngster is taught how to handle and care for his pet in a very gentle manner.

these rodents is *Cavia porcellus*, the latter term deriving from the Latin *porcus*, meaning a hog or swine.

The alternative common name of cavy probably derives from the scientific name of *Cavia*, which is Latin for a hollow or cave and was first applied by the German zoolo-gist Professor Pallas in 1766.

THE GUINEA PIG AND ITS RELATIVES

The guinea pig is a member of the order of mammals called Rodentia, the rodents. This is the largest group in the class of animals known as mammals—those that suckle their young and have hairy bodies. Rodents are characterized by their gnawing incisor teeth, which grow continually throughout their lives.

The order Rodentia is divided into various groups (suborders), one of which is called Hystricomorpha, the porcupine-like rodents. Guinea pigs are in this group. The suborder is divided into numerous families, the guinea pigs being in that called Caviidae.

There are five subdivisions within Caviidae, each of which is called a genus. Our interest is in that known as *Cavia*, the cavies, or guinea pigs. At genus level, the members in it (called species) are quite closely related. This is apparent by their similar appearance. However, each species is different enough to warrant being placed in its specific group.

Although the guinea pig that you will see in pet shops has the scientific name of *Cavia porcellus*, it is not thought to be a naturally wild species. Current thinking is that it is either the domesticated form of a single wild species or a hybrid of two or three of them, the candidates

The domestication of the guinea pig, *Cavia porcellus*, began about 3,000 years ago in South America.

There are several breeds of guinea pig in a wide variety of colors and markings. This is a tri-color version.

crepuscular, meaning that their activity is generally during the twilight hours. But they are known to forage during daylight hours when food is scarce. They are terrestrial, having no ability to climb other than to scamper over small rocks.

They live in a range of habitats, which comprise grasslands, edges of forests, rocky regions, even swamplands. They form family groups of four to ten individuals headed by a dominant boar, his harem of females, and young males. Family groups may share a territory, giving the impression that they live in large colonies.

The diet is a wide range of vegetation. Cavies are unusual in that they, like humans and other primates (monkeys and apes), are unable to synthesize vitamin C in their bodies—it must come via their food.

being *C. aperea*, *C. fulgida*, and *C.tschudii*.

In this sense, the guinea pig compares with domestic dogs and cats, both of which are domesticated variants of a wild species. They are given full species status because they existed in their present form long before humans started to document species, so their true origin is uncertain.

WILD-CAVY LIFESTYLE
Cavies are basically

CAVIES AS PETS
Although not as popular as rabbits, guinea pigs can make equally desirable pets. They are more timid than rabbits, so they are best suited to families in which any children are at the age of reason and can understand the need to handle and care for these animals in a very gentle manner. They are very clean animals with no body odor. They are easy to feed and house, and they rarely bite.

They have an average weight of two pounds and are available in a number of breeds that feature a wide range of color patterns. Longevity is about four to six years, but they have been known to reach eight years, though this is rare.

Guinea pigs are social animals that enjoy the company of their own kind. Owning a pair of guinea pigs is hardly any more work than owning just one, and they can keep each other company when you are not home.

A golden-and-white guinea pig. Through selective breeding, many attractive color patterns have been developed, and no doubt new ones will be seen in the future.

A young Teddy. The distinguishing feature of this breed is the short, curly coat, which, ideally, should be dense and resilient.

CHOOSING YOUR GUINEA PIG

When thinking about owning a guinea pig as a pet, your first consideration should be whether you are the kind of person who will totally commit yourself to this little mammal for the four to six years that it will live with you. All too often, pets, those of low cost in particular, are purchased on an impulse only to be neglected when their novelty has worn off.

Never purchase a guinea pig for a child unless you are prepared to attend to all of its needs once the child loses interest, as many will. Your new pet will require daily handling if it is to remain a very friendly companion. If space and money permit, purchase two or more females who will provide each other with company when you are not at home. Alternatively, a *small* rabbit breed will make a super companion for a guinea pig: both are very social animals by nature.

Keeping a male and a female guinea pig is not a good idea because they will quickly start breeding and present you with (possibly) unwanted babies. Two males are also not the best choice if they are to live together. They may start to fight when mature.

PURCHASE AGE

Cavies are normally weaned at about four weeks of age, so any time after this is a good age at which to obtain one. Usually, youngsters are the best to purchase because they are cute and fun when at this age. However, if you have children under the age of about ten, your pet shop may have a tame young adult.

This might be a better choice in this instance. Very young children cannot reliably handle a guinea pig, so it is wiser to have one that is strong and robust. Even so, you must always supervise young children; otherwise, they may lift and then drop the guinea pig, with considerable risk that it may be badly hurt. Guinea pigs have short slim legs that are easily injured.

FUR TYPE

A major consideration with these pets will be their fur type. There are both shorthaired and longhaired breeds. The shorthaired versions are normally the best choice for the average family. Their coats are sleek and full of sheen. They require minimal grooming. Longhaired breeds need a lot of time devoted to them. Their fur can quickly become a mess if it is neglected.

An alternative to the shorthaired breeds would be the teddy, whose coat is still short but is coarse and kinked. The other shortcoated breed is the Abyssinian, with its rosettes and ridges of fur. Pet shops usually have a range of guinea pigs displaying the various

Teddy and Peruvian guinea pigs. The fur type of your prospective guinea pig is an important consideration. The longhair varieties require a considerable amount of grooming to keep their coats in good condition.

coat types. If you want a purebred guinea pig of a particular breed, you will have to pay more for it, the amount being determined by the breed, its color rarity, and quality.

COAT COLOR

Although this should not be a determining factor in choosing a good pet guinea pig, it often can be. Most people have color preferences. There is a wide choice of colors and patterns in this pet, but health

A healthy guinea pig will have bright, clear eyes with no signs of weeping. Its nose will be dry to moist, with no signs of discharge.

and fur type should always be your main concerns.

HEALTH

Good health is the most important consideration in any pet. Your future enjoyment will be dependent on this, so never accept any guinea pig that is less than 100 percent fit. Your assessment of good health should begin with the conditions under which the pet is living. They will tell you a great deal about the way it is being cared for.

It should be in a clean, spacious cage or pen, having adequate water and food. It should not be living in crowded conditions, and the sexes should not be mixed. Satisfied on these aspects, you should select one or two specimens that appeal to you and then carefully observe them. Yours will be one of those displaying no undue fears at your proximity to its home. It should be active, not one that is sitting in the corner with little interest in what is going on around it.

The salesperson should

hold the guinea pig so that you can inspect it more closely. Its eyes should be bright and fully open with no signs of weeping. The nostrils will be dry to just moist—never runny or swollen. The ears have a natural crinkle and are partially pendulous.

The coat in shorthaired varieties is sleek and smooth; that in the Abyssinian is rough. There should be no signs of sores or bald spots, nor any areas devoid of hair. Inspect the anal region, which should be clean, showing no indication of fecal staining suggestive of

Very young children should be supervised when spending time with the family guinea pig. Guinea pigs are rather timid and abrupt movements can frighten them.

present or recent diarrhea.

The front feet have four digits, the rear three. The sexes have only two mammary glands. The body should be well muscled, not obese or too thin, though in very young guinea pigs it will

not have the substance of a mature individual.

It is very important to check the teeth to ensure that they are correctly aligned. The upper incisors should just overlap, but touch, those of the lower jaw. By grinding them one against the other, the teeth stay at the required length—assuming the pet has something hard on which to gnaw as well. This self-regulating process is not possible if the teeth are misaligned (malocclusion) or if an incisor should break. In either instance, veterinary attention is required. Do not purchase a guinea pig whose teeth are already obviously excessively long, or other than well aligned.

QUESTIONS TO ASK

Having selected your pet guinea pig, you should make a note on the feeding regimen of the pet store. You should ask what age the guinea pig is and establish if it comes with any sort of guarantee, and how long this is good for. A good supplier will give you this information in writing.

THE FIRST DAYS IN YOUR HOME

When any young animal moves into its new home, it is a very stressful period. You must make things as easy as possible for the guinea pig. This is very important with shy creatures like guinea pigs. If a guinea pig becomes unduly stressed, this will lower its ability to utilize the vitamin C content of its diet.

Transport the guinea pig home in a well-ventilated box filled with hay and maybe a few food pellets. Once it is home, place the pet in its new housing, which ideally will have been obtained before the guinea pig was purchased. Let it explore its housing before you start to handle it. This gives it time to settle down and maybe have a short rest.

Children *must* be taught to respect the privacy of their pet and not constantly be disturbing it when it is sleeping. You must also show them how to handle their companion so that it will not be in danger of being dropped or otherwise injured.

HANDLING

Unless the guinea pig is already hand tame, it may display some initial fear of being handled. Never startle your pet as you approach it: do everything slowly and in such a way that the guinea pig is aware of your presence and your hands. It will probably scurry to a corner, at which time you can place one hand over its shoulders to steady it, placing the other hand under its body. It is important that its total weight is always supported by one hand; otherwise, it will feel insecure and start to wriggle. Never grasp it around its shoulders and lift so that its rear end is dangling unsupported.

Once lifted, you can bring it close to your chest and rest its underparts on your arm. This is more difficult with a youngster, so it is best to sit down. It can rest in your lap until it is older and familiar with being handled.

CAVIES AND OTHER PETS

Cavies will get along fine with rabbits, provided that they are one of the smaller breeds. Other pets, such as dogs, cats, ferrets, and even the newer pets such as the hedgehog, are another matter. Generally, it is wise to keep your guinea pig away from them. Cats in particular may decide that the guinea pig is a potential snack or at least something that can be attacked, even if only in a playful manner.

Dogs may become too rough

In addition to removing mats and tangles, brushing also helps to evenly distribute the coat's natural oils.

in trying to play with a guinea pig, while ferrets will view the guinea pig as a prey species. You will of course hear of people whose dogs and cats just love their guinea pig, but those whose pet has been killed or badly injured by these other pets will generally not boast about it. Play it safe and keep the guinea pig safe.

HOME SECURITY

You are probably going to allow your pet free access to one or more rooms in your home. This being so, a few safety tips are prudent. In warm weather, be careful that doors are not subject to drafts that might slam them on the pet as it moves from one room to another. Be sure that exterior doors are closed when the guinea pig is free roaming.

Indoor plants should never be at floor level where the pet might nibble on them: some plants may be toxic to a guinea pig. Trailing electrical wires could be a source of danger if nibbled. Check each room to ensure that the guinea pig cannot get into a place in which you might have trouble retrieving it or where other dangers, such as open fires, might be present.

When exercising a guinea pig in your garden, do not give it access to flower beds that may have been sprayed with toxic chemicals, nor where other animals may have fouled the area with fecal matter.

When outdoors, a guinea pig should *never* be left unsupervised. It has many potential enemies, such as dogs, cats, birds of prey, foxes, and coyotes. Remind your children of this.

If you observe all of these guidelines, you will obtain a little guinea pig that will be a delight to own. Guinea pigs soon learn to recognize your voice and will squeak and whistle with delight when it is dinner time. They are very friendly little pets and respond well to gentle handling and the quieter home.

HOUSING

Guinea pigs can be housed in a range of accommodations produced commercially for rabbits and other small mammals. Good pet shops will have a selection from which to choose. Visit a number of stores to see the widest range possible. The major requirements of good housing are that it is spacious, sturdy, secure, and easy to keep clean.

SIZE

The rule for guinea pig housing is that it should be as large as your finances will permit. The minimum size should be about 62 x 38cm (24 x 15 in.). Such a cage will provide only room for sleeping and feeding. You must give your pet ample time outside of its cage. If two guinea pigs are to share the housing, its size should be increased by about 20 percent.

HOUSE STYLES

The range of styles from which you can choose is almost bewildering. There are all-glass aquarium style cages made specifically for small mammals. The largest of them would be suitable for a guinea pig, but most owners prefer wire cages for these pets.

Wire cages range from the modestly priced to expensive, depending on their features and the way the wire is coated. They may be galvanized, epoxy coated, or chromium plated. Some feature exercise wheels and feed/water pots; others do not. Some have wire floors to allow

fecal matter to fall onto a receiving tray below; others have solid floors.

One of the problems arising with wire-mesh floors is that they can be very uncomfortable for the pet's feet. One style available largely overcomes this by featuring transverse plastic bars that provide a much larger and softer surface area for the pet's feet yet allow fecal matter to fall through the gaps between the bars.

Another method of making things more comfortable is to feature wire mesh in one area, which, hopefully, the pet will use as a toilet, the rest of the floor being solid. The guinea pig has small feet. Therefore, it is important that if mesh

Make sure that you have a secure grip on your pet when putting it into its cage. Some guinea pigs have been known to struggle free and in so doing cause injury to their teeth and claws.

Here, the cage is being placed over a cat litter pan, which will catch the guinea pig's waste matter. The pan has been lined with wood shavings to absorb urine.

floors are a feature, there must be no danger of its nails getting tangled on the wire.

This author prefers solid-floor cages for these pets. They are more comfortable, allow a generous layer of bedding to be used, and are clearly a more natural surface on which to walk.

You can obtain two-and three-story cages that considerably increase the floor area for your pet without taking up more ground space in the home. Alternatively, there are long-unit cages equipped with insert/divider panels to increase or reduce the space according to need. These are popular with rabbit and guinea pig breeders.

Wooden hutches as used by rabbit breeders of past years have largely been supplanted by the more airy and readily cleaned cages discussed.

HOUSE FURNISHINGS

Your guinea pig's home will need a generous layer of floor-

Cage accessories include a gravity-fed water bottle and a sturdy non-tippable food bowl.

covering material, food and water pots, and a nestbox or other retreat area. An exercise wheel is a useful addition. In a very large unit, additional furnishings would be a slate or granite rock to give aesthetic appeal and provide something with which the guinea pig can amuse itself.

FLOOR COVERING

The choices for floor covering include white pine shavings, corncob, natural wood or grass fiber, and hay. Avoid cedar shavings because the phenols in them are harmful to your guinea pig's respiratory system. Sawdust is too fine and can create problems if it clings to the anogenital region or the swollen teats of a nursing sow. Straw has little absorbency, and its sharp ends can be injurious to the eyes of these pets.

Sheets of paper and granulated paper have good absorbency but are aesthetically

unattractive. The ink in newsprint is potentially harmful. Paper sheets under other bedding materials is a method used by some owners.

Corncob is a popular choice but lacks good absorbency. Wood fiber is one of the safest beddings, but it is rather expensive. Hay is a natural bedding and is one that the pet can also eat. However, when damp from urine, water, or fecal matter, it may quickly spawn fungi. This is its biggest drawback, along with the fact that it has limited absorbency.

This leaves us with shavings as the most popular and economical bedding at this time. *Never* obtain shavings from saw mills or lumberyards. They may contain mites and other unwanted parasites. Purchase commercially bagged shavings from your pet shop. Some are impregnated with chlorophyll (giving a green color) to reduce odors and make them more attractive.

This well-appointed cage even includes a hay rack, which is attached to its side. When selecting a cage, choose one that will allow your pet to move around comfortably.

You will find that some shavings are more dust free than others—their extra cost is worth it on this account. The depth of bedding should be about 5cm (2 in.).

NESTBOX OR OTHER RETREAT

Guinea pigs are very shy creatures. In the wild, they keep a low profile by retreating behind rocks, in bushes, or under leaves when resting or sleeping. If this need to retreat is not met, it will greatly increase their stress level, making them more susceptible to illness.

You can easily overcome this risk by providing a small nestbox or similar hiding place. You can purchase nestboxes from pet stores. Stores will also sell appropriately sized plastic tubes secured onto a flat plastic base, or those creating small tunnels. These will work fine and provide amusement for your guinea pig.

EXERCISE WHEEL

Exercise wheels are very useful appliances for guinea pigs, but they must be large enough and safe. Avoid those with open treads, through which legs can easily become trapped. You need one with a solid non-slip floor. It should be sturdy, so that it will not easily topple over. Always remember that it pays to invest in the best cage accessories. They are safer and will give you much longer wear.

LOCATION OF THE CAGE

Your guinea pig's cage should be located in a place appropriate for the pet's needs as well as yours. Never place it where it will be subject to strong sunlight—such as on a

Above: Wooden housing is not a suitable choice for guinea pigs or other small-mammal pets. It is subject to the pet's gnawing and will also retain urine odor. *Below:* Play time. These guinea pigs have been provided with a portable outdoor enclosure that allows plenty of room for exercise and the opportunity to nibble on some grass.

window sill. Nor should it be facing doors where it could easily receive a draft during the colder months. Another poor location for the cage is over a radiator. There will be a temperature fluctuation as the appliances go on and off. This could easily induce chills. The choice should be where it is light and airy, where the temperature will be the most stable, yet where you can easily attend routine chores and observe your pet without any inconvenience.

OUTDOOR EXERCISE FACILITY

Many owners ask if it is safe to allow their guinea pig outdoor exercise time in their yard. The answer is yes: The pet will enjoy the fresh air. However, a few precautions are required.

You need to provide a secure pen that restricts the guinea pig from wandering away and will not allow potential intruders, such as dogs or cats, to enter the pen. This is easily done by covering it with weldwire. The pen should be located on a flat surface so that there are no escape holes. Guinea pigs are poor burrowers, so they will not try to dig their way under the sides.

The pen should be situated where it will receive some sunshine yet always have a shaded area or retreat. This is *very* important. Also be sure that your pet has access to water at all times. On warm spring, summer, and autumn days, your pet(s) will enjoy scampering about a large exercise pen. It can be equipped with rocks and plastic tunnels. You will be fascinated watching your pets as they scamper around with obvious curiosity and enjoyment.

If you choose to allow your guinea pig time outdoors, be sure to stay nearby so that it is not threatened by any stray animals.

CONTROLLING GUINEA PIG ODORS

More than at any other time in the history of these pets, guinea pigs are being kept in the home, rather than under outbuilding conditions. The reason is related to the fact that commercial housing options are now better than ever before, coupled with better bedding options and improved odor removers.

Under home conditions, you are able to interact far more readily with your pet. As a consequence, you are better able to appreciate some of the qualities of the guinea pig often not appreciated when interaction time is limited. Another beneficial side effect of housing your guinea pig in your home is that your pet will probably get more attention than might be the case if it lives away from you. The downside of "out of sight out of mind" is less likely to be applicable.

However, success in maintaining a guinea pig in your home will be very dependent on your ability to control pet-related odors. The subject is therefore worthy of this special chapter.

HOW ODORS ARE CAUSED

All animals create odors in two ways. The first is their natural body odor. This should present no problem to you because guinea pigs do not have an unpleasant smell. They keep themselves clean by self grooming. You can help the process by regularly grooming your pet as well. Use a soft bristle brush followed by a polish with a chamois, leather, or silk cloth.

The more obvious source of unpleasant odors is fecal matter and urine. What happens is that bacteria break down undigested foods and waste matter present in the

Your guinea pig's housing and its furnishings should be cleaned weekly.

feces. This process, known as the nitrogen cycle, creates ammonia gas and other compounds, which are what create the noxious odors.

Additionally, fresh foods that are left too long in the housing are also subject to this process, as is the bedding itself once it is dampened by urine, and even spilled water. Control this part of the nitrogen cycle and you control offensive odors.

CONTROLLING NOXIOUS ODORS

There are a number of ways that pet owners can control odor. The least worthwhile is to spray pleasant scents over them—air fresheners and their like. These products have a rapid initial action but are quickly ineffective because they do nothing to the actual molecules causing the smell.

Regular cleaning of the housing is obviously the best way to control odors because you remove the source—soiled bedding and the fecal matter itself. The amount of times per week that you will need to clean your guinea pig's home will depend on how large its cage is, the type of housing, and the number of guinea pigs in the cage.

There are two types of cleaning. One is the daily removal of obvious areas of fecal matter or water spillage. These should be topped over with fresh bedding. There is then complete cage cleaning. This should be done every seven days at the latest, more often with smaller housing. Food and water vessels should be cleaned daily. The *entire* cage and its furnishings should be cleaned weekly. It is especially important that the cage corners are well cleaned. A dilute solution of bleach (not general household disinfectants) will kill most bacteria and fungi. Be very sure to rinse the cage thoroughly after using bleach. Allow the cage to dry completely.

Your second way to greatly

reduce odors is to use one of the modern preparations that break down waste material by enzymatic action. Such products are available at pet shops.

A third way to combat odors is to feature a mineral that will neutralize the ammonium compounds by converting them into inert non-odorous compounds. Zeolite is very familiar to aquarists for this purpose. It is now gaining popularity with non-aquarists. Zeolite chips can be placed into plastic tubs with holes, and the tubs can then be placed in or near the cage. Zeolite chips have a highly absorbent surface. When they are saturated with the new compound formed from the ammonia, they will no longer be effective. At this time they can be soaked for 24 hours in a saline solution, which will release the unwanted compounds, enabling the zeolite to be used again. Charcoal chips also have highly adsorptive surfaces that will neutralize some odors, but the charcoal is not "rechargeable."

A mechanical means of minimizing odors is to feature an ionizer in the room in which the guinea pig lives. These appliances are popular with bird breeders. They range in size, depending on the area over which they are meant to be effective. They release millions of negative ions that attract dust and bacteria, as well as molecules of odorous substances, making the molecules heavier than air so that they fall to the floor or other surfaces. They are removed with daily cleaning.

When you are trying to eliminate odors, bear in mind that their molecules can travel some distance from a cage. It is prudent to use odor neutralizers on carpets and other absorbent surfaces. However, *never* rely on such products to replace the basic need to use regular cleaning as the prime way to remove odors. This is poor husbandry practice.

LITTER BOX TRAINING

The fact that your guinea pig is a herbivore limits its potential to ever be as houseclean as a carnivore—such as a dog, cat, or ferret.

This is because its digestive

Straw is not a good choice for floor covering. It is not absorbent, and the sharp ends can cause eye injuries.

tract should always be processing a steady flow of food. This means that fecal matter is being expelled at a steady rate. Carnivores eat larger meals and defecate less frequently than herbivores. They are easier to litter box train. In the wild, they will often try to hide their fecal matter to mask their presence. Herbivores do not do this.

Success at litter box training in the home means that you must bear in mind that your guinea pig has far less control over its bowel movements than does your dog or cat. A guinea pig will not travel very far in order to use a litter box, even though it does like to use one location as a toilet area in its cage.

Success at house training a guinea pig should be based on the following guidelines:

1. Do not let your pet have free access to all rooms until its litter box training is under control.

2. Start in a room such as the kitchen, where it is easy to keep the floor free of odors that might attract the pet to given locations—which might be the case in carpeted rooms.

3. Place two or three litter boxes at convenient locations in the room so that the pet does not have to travel far to reach one. Place a few fecal droppings and urine-stained floor covering in the litter box so that the guinea pig is

reminded that this is a toilet area.

4. Ensure that the litter box is easy to enter and large enough for your pet to turn around in.

Silkie. This guinea pig has had its long coat trimmed for ease of grooming. How clean your guinea pig is will largely depend on your husbandry methods.

5. If the pet is seen to use a particular location, rather than its litter box, move the box to that spot. Even if you have success at

litter box training, it will never be 100 percent. You must accept the fact that some fecal matter will be dropped in the room, but guinea pig pellets are small, soon go hard, and are easily swept up. If you expect your pet to be perfect in its toiletry habits, you are expecting too much.

If you find that your pet is fouling a difficult-to-reach area of a particular room, the best advice is to keep the pet out of that room for a given time period—a few weeks would be appropriate. This allows time for you to completely remove any odors from that room, and your pet might stop finding random toilet sites in it.

By applying a combination of thorough cleanliness of your guinea pig's cage along with the utilization of modern odor controllers, obnoxious smells will be a thing of the past.

A lovely pair of Abyssinian guinea pigs. This breed is distinguished by the whorls of fur, known as rosettes, on its body.

Guinea pigs need to be bathed only on an occasional basis. This procedure should be performed in a draft-free area. Use a mild shampoo formulated for animals.

NUTRITION

Guinea pigs are herbivores. This means that their diet consists exclusively of plant and vegetable matter. It is essential that they have a high-fiber, low-fat-content diet rich in vitamin C, which cannot be synthesized by guinea pigs as it can by all other mammals excluding primates. Any deficiency will result in poor health.

The components of a healthy guinea pig's diet should include unlimited fresh hay, fresh leafy greens, guinea pig pellets, some vegetables and fruits, and fresh water. Any other foods should be regarded as nonessential and supplied as treats on a limited basis. Before discussing diet items, we will look at feeding-related topics.

FOOD AND WATER CONTAINERS

Food can be supplied in two crock pots: one for pellets and other dried foods, the other for fresh vegetables and fruits. The pots are available from your local pet store. Crock is best because it is not as easily tipped by guinea pigs as is plastic or aluminum.

Water can be supplied in gravity-fed water bottles or open crock pots. Water bottles have the advantage that the water remains clean and free from fouling by dust or bedding material. The disadvantage is that it takes your pet a long time to drink sufficiently to satiate it.

Open pots provide water in a more natural manner, but some fouling is inevitable, necessitating daily cleaning. This of course ensures that the water is fresh. If a bottle is used, be sure to obtain one of the better models to reduce the risk of water leaking—one with a metal tip is preferred.

Position the bottle so that it is easily reached by your guinea pig.

WHEN TO FEED

Fresh hay should be available at all times. Pellets and other dried foods can normally be left in dishes until eaten.

Fresh water should be available to your guinea pig at all times.

They do not deteriorate very quickly and are minimally attractive to flies and other insects. Fresh (moist) foods are the ones that should therefore be given at special times.

These foods have a very limited exposure life, quickly souring if not eaten within a few hours. After such periods, any that is left should be removed and thrown out. It is best to feed fresh foods early in the day, or in the late afternoon/early evening, when it is normally a little cooler and you are able to devote more time to your guinea pig.

HOW MUCH TO FEED?

Guinea pigs need sufficient food to meet their health and activity level. A large pet will clearly eat more than will a small one. An active guinea pig given plenty of exercise

Hay is part of a guinea pig's diet. It provides the roughage that aids in digestion.

When introducing new foods, do so gradually. Sudden changes in diet can cause diarrhea and other gastrointestinal problems.

FEEDING-RELATED PROBLEMS

The most serious problems seen in pet guinea pigs today are obesity, scurvy, and gastrointestinal-related problems and diseases. These are usually the result of incorrect diets and poorly regulated feeding regimens.

It is very important that diets are not suddenly changed from one food type to another. For example, if a guinea pig has basically been on a pellet and grain diet, with insufficient fresh plant matter and hay, and these latter two items are suddenly supplied in quantity, chances are high that problems will result.

The reason is that pellets and grain foods are very high in calories and low in fiber. They slow down the digestive rate. When fresh foods are supplied, the digestive system increases its speed to the required level.

This, and changes in the type of gut flora required for each food type, result in temporary digestive disruption that often shows itself in the condition commonly referred to as scouring, or acute diarrhea. This condition can prove fatal in young stock, but is avoidable if the owner feeds his guinea pig in a sensible manner.

BALANCED FEEDING IS ESSENTIAL

When you obtain your guinea pig, be sure to ask what its present diet is. If it is not balanced, which we will discuss shortly, make changes *gradually*. This will enable the pet's digestive system to slowly adjust to the new feeding regimen. Problems, if any, will be minor and should clear up within a few days.

A balanced diet is one that provides those ingredients known to be important to the health of a pet, and supplied in a quantity or ratio one to the other that allows them to be digested in a manner that will not result in subsequent problems. When a new food item is added to the diet, it must *never* be added in a glut just because the guinea pig shows a liking for it or because it becomes seasonably available—as with wild plants.

This same comment even applies to foods that the pet is already familiar with. For example, your guinea pig may enjoy a small piece of apple as a treat. But do not suddenly give it a quantity in excess of that which is normal for it. If

Guinea pigs are herbivorous, which means that their diet consists exclusively of plant and vegetable matter.

facility will burn up more energy than will one in a small cage. A nursing female needs more than a non-bred female.

Given these different needs, and the fact that some foods are more nutritious than others, it is not possible to state exact amounts to feed. The best way to determine quantity is to supply a given amount of pellets, mixed grain, and fresh foods (plus unlimited hay) and see how much of it is eaten within a few hours.

If all or most is eaten, you can increase the quantity of those items completely eaten at the next meal. If a lot is left, you can reduce the amount. The ideal situation is that in which the guinea pig eats most of its food, but some is left to be eaten later. By such an adjustment method, you will soon arrive at the optimum for good health and minimal waste.

you do, an upset stomach may well be the result. You must carefully administrate what children give to their pets. They have a habit of supplying too much of an item because the pet clearly enjoys it. Never feed sweet, stodgy foods, such as candies and other junk items. They have no benefit at all.

THE BASIC DIET INGREDIENTS

Hay: This dietary item should be available at all times. It enables the digestive system to work as it should. It is especially beneficial to longhaired breeds in helping to prevent hairballs, and to all guinea pigs in helping to minimize the risk of diarrhea and its related problems.

There are numerous types of hay. You should purchase mixed grass hay, timothy, or oat hay. Alfalfa is acceptable but is rather richer in calories and calcium. It is important that the hay is fresh. That which is produced commercially for pet shops is excellent. Never feed hay that looks "off" or smells other than fresh. It will cause stomach upsets. Store hay in a cool dry area that is well ventilated to avoid fungal spores from developing.

Pellets: Pelleted food has the advantage of convenience and is rich in important nutrients. Because the pellets are in a dried form, they are very concentrated; so it is easy to feed excess amounts. Be sure the pellets are those fortified with

vitamin C. Do not purchase excess amounts. The vitamin C content deteriorates significantly by the end of 60 days as a result of exposure to air, dampness, and heat. Store in a well-ventilated but dry, cool cupboard. Keep the bag sealed after each use. As a general guide, feed about 0.75 oz. (21g), or one-eighth of a cup per day to the average-weight pet (2 lbs.), adjusting according to size and weight.

Plants and vegetables: The vitamin C and fiber content of green leaf plants make them excellent supplements to hay and pellets. They also provide high moisture content. The leaves of green vegetables such as cabbage, parsley, turnip, and carrot tops are examples. Dandelion is a wild plant that guinea pigs enjoy (leaves and flower). Other plants that you can supply are spinach, shepherd's purse, groundsel, chickweed, plantain, bramble, clover, coltsfoot, mallow, and chard. Lettuce, a long-time favored item with some rabbit and guinea pig breeders, actually has little nutritional value and is overrated.

Guinea pigs will enjoy a range of fruits and vegetables, such as apples, carrots, pea pods, and grapes. The importance of not feeding any of these foods in excess cannot be overstressed. It is also wise to rinse all plants, vegetables, and fruits to remove residual chemicals used in crop spraying. If you are unsure about a particular wild plant, do not feed it. Never feed any plant grown from a bulb.

Pet shops carry a variety of guinea pig treat foods that your pet will enjoy. Photo courtesy of Kaytee.

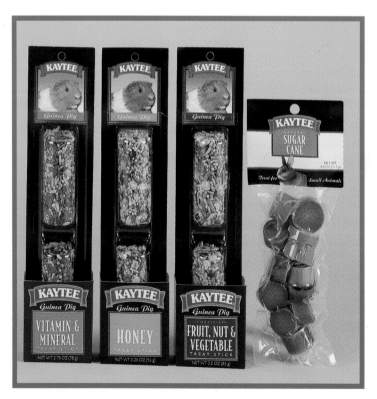

Seed, grain, and their byproducts: Many cereal crops, together with seeds such as canary, sunflower, and panicum, will be eaten by guinea pigs. As with many food items, your pet may be selective.

If you are feeding hay, pellets, and mixed plants, care should be exercised in the feeding of high-protein and high-carbohydrate seeds and grain. Obesity might become a problem. Reduce the quantity of pellets when feeding seed and grain.

Baked bread, pellets, and small branches of fruit and other edible trees are required to ensure that your pet's teeth stay at the required length. If a guinea pig does not have sufficient, hard items on which to gnaw, its incisor teeth will grow to an excessive length, which creates major problems.

Above: The piece of carrot that this guinea pig is eating is far too big a portion. Fruits and vegetables are *supplements* to a guinea pig diet, not the mainstay. *Below:* The pelleted food in your guinea pig's diet must be one that is specially formulated for guinea pigs. Such foods are fortified with vitamin C, which a guinea pig cannot synthesize on its own. Photo courtesy of Kaytee.

You should regularly check to see that the incisors are being kept at a suitable length. If you see either the top or bottom teeth getting too long, consult your vet right away. The teeth can be trimmed, and you can adjust the diet to provide the correct food items. If you ignore this advice, the teeth may grow into the opposite jaw, or curl outside the mouth, making it impossible for the pet to eat.

WATCH YOUR PET WHILE IT IS EATING

Always take the time to watch your guinea pig when it is eating. You will learn much about its habits. Any change in these habits may be the first sign of a problem. Some pets are greedy feeders; others are dainty. A pet that refuses a favorite item suggests a problem.

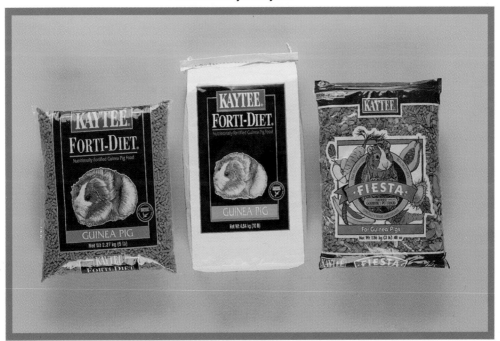

it will display an obviously healthy coat. If your guinea pig does not present this kind of appearance, you should seek veterinary advice.

VITAMIN AND MINERAL SUPPLEMENTS

If your guinea pig is eating a varied, well-balanced diet and is in good health, the addition of extra vitamins and minerals could create problems. Vitamins and minerals should be supplied only under the advice of a vet after he has examined your pet.

Above: A guinea pig's teeth grow continuously throughout the animal's lifetime. If a guinea pig does not have hard items on which it can gnaw, its incisor teeth will grow excessively long. Oodles®, manufactured by the Nylabone Corporation, are a very effective means to help keep your pet's teeth to the proper length. *Below:* For variety, you can offer your guinea pig flavored Oodles®.

One that is suddenly eating or drinking more than usual may also have a problem. Of course, a pregnant female or a pet recovering from an illness would be expected to eat and drink more than a nonbreeding individual.

If your pet is receiving a balanced diet, it will display good body substance, being neither fat nor thin. It will be alert and active—the guinea pig is also known as the restless guinea pig—and

This guinea pig is fed a good diet. It is healthy looking and its weight is just right.

BREEDING & EXHIBITION

The best advice that a pet owner can take with regard to breeding is that he should leave it well alone. It is an area of the hobby better left to dedicated enthusiasts who specialize in producing purebred guinea pigs. There is no shortage of these pets, nor of breeders.

Pet shops are continually turning away unwanted mixed-breed guinea pig youngsters produced by pet owners, so why add to the existing excess supply? If you think you would like to be a breeder and/or exhibitor, the following will provide a basic primer to the subject.

first pet(s) will fall far short of the quality needed upon which to base a breeding program. You will need stock that can be registered with your national guinea pig association. The guinea pigs that you select should be pedigreed and carry a

When breeding guinea pigs, select only those specimens that are in top condition. Unfit guinea pigs will likely produce young that will be prone to problems.

trated when things do not go as anticipated. Plan every aspect before you start.

MAKING A START

Do not be tempted to start with too many individuals. Keep things low key, gradually expanding your breeding program in ratio to your ability to successfully manage it. You will need only one good boar and two or three nice sows to get underway. The boar should be the best that you can afford because he will be spreading his genes via *each* of the sows.

The sows can be distantly related or unrelated. As a beginner, it is probably best that you start with proven breeding stock—that which has bred previously and produced healthy babies. This reduces the risk of problems that may occur when unproven individuals are obtained. At the least, the boar should be a known producer.

INITIAL CONSIDERATIONS

The first prerequisite for a potential breeder is that he gains practical husbandry experience in managing these pets. As he does so, information pertinent to breeding can be gathered. A breeder should be acquainted with all the guinea pig breeds and their color patterns so that he can start with one that appeals to him and presents the least problems to manage.

It is probable that your

permanent identification eartag, tattoo, or legband, depending on the regulations of the country in which you live.

Breeding takes up a lot of time and requires extra cash—for food and especially for the additional cages that you will need. Be sure that you have these resources and also the space needed for the increasing number of guinea pigs that you will own. It is very easy to rush into breeding and become frus-

BREEDING FACTS

Sexing: This can be done only by inspection of the genital organs situated in front of the anus. Rest the guinea pig on its back in the palm of your hand. Use the free hand (or have a helper) to gently apply pressure on either side of the genital opening. This will result in the extrusion of the penis in the male. The female has a membrane covering the genital orifice.

In a mature boar, the testes of the male will make matters more obvious. Both sexes display teats, of which there should be just two.

Sexual maturity: A female guinea pig may attain sexual maturity as early as 21 days of age. This is far too young for her to be bred. This should be done when she is about three months old but not later than six months for her first litter; otherwise, she may have difficulty during parturition (the birthing process).

A boar should be about five to six months old before he is bred, even though he is capable of mating from the tender age of about three to four weeks of age. Breeding guinea pigs that are not physically mature greatly increases the possibility of producing weak offspring, as well as stunting the growth maturity of the sow in particular.

Estrus cycle: This is the time it takes for a female's sexual arousal to commence and end. It is about 13-17 days in guinea pigs. Actual mating will take place some days into the cycle, when the female is at her estrus peak.

Mating method: A boar can be left with one to ten females for mating, or you can use a single sow if you want just a particular female to be bred. Place the female with the boar. You may leave her with him for only a limited time if matings are seen, for a few days, or even a few weeks. The sow must be removed before she has her litter and placed back in her own cage, which should be supplied with a nestbox. It is not that the boar will normally harm the babies but because the sow has an estrus just after birthing and will be mated again if the boar is present. During the general mating excitement, the newborns could be injured.

Gestation period: This is the time between fertilization of the sow's eggs and the birth of the litter. The period is normally about 68 days, though the potential range for the species is 56-74 days. Births toward the upper limits would normally be dead or have problems.

Litter size: An average litter will comprise 2 to 4 babies, but as many as 13 has been recorded. Large litters usually result in a number of infant deaths. The sow has but two nipples with which to feed the babies, but average litters all get their share of the milk.

Condition of the young at birth: Cavies are born fully furred with their eyes open, and they are able to run around within minutes. They are able to nibble at solid foods within 24-36 hours.

Weaning: This has normally taken place by the time the youngsters are three to four weeks of age. At this time, boars should be removed from the litter to prevent the risk of premature breeding with their sisters, or even their mother.

If longhaired varieties are bred, it is wise to trim the hair to a shorter length so that there is no risk that it will interfere with mating (getting around the male's penis) or create birthing or

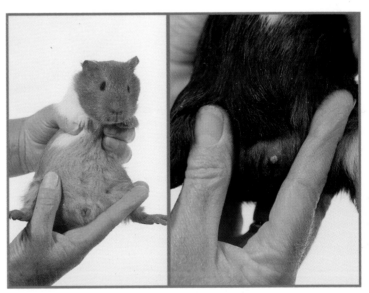

Sexing guinea pigs. Gentle pressure on both sides of the genital area will reveal the penis of the male. If there is no penis, then obviously it is a female.

feeding problems for the female and her babies.

Breeding life: A sow will usually end her breeding life when she is about three years old, though exceptions are not rare. A male will remain fertile for a longer period, but litter size and vigor may be reduced as he gets older.

EXHIBITING GUINEA PIGS

The guinea pig show is the shop window to the entire hobby. At a large show, you will see every breed, and probably every available color and pattern. New guinea pig products are displayed at shows, and current trends and knowledge are exchanged between breeders. The exhibition side of the hobby is a hobby unto itself.

Guinea pigs are exhibited in a variety of classes based on sex, age, weight, breed, and, finally, color and pattern. Winners from each of

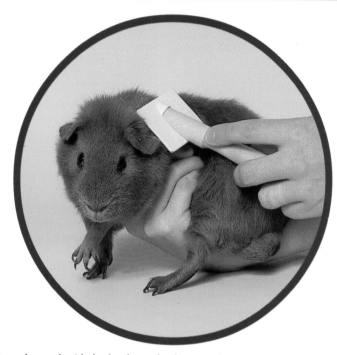

Grooming a short-haired guinea pig. An occasional brushing will remove loose hair. Brush gently—guinea pigs have sensitive skin—working from head to rump.

these groups progress through the show until a best-in-show is declared.

To be eligible for competition, a guinea pig must be registered with the association that is organizing the show, must have a three-generation pedigree, a permanent mark of identification (eartag, tattoo, or legband), and be a sound example of its breed and variety. It is judged against the standard of excellence of the ruling association.

The standard of quality in show guinea pigs is extremely high at major exhibitions. It takes a great deal of work to maintain an exhibition guinea pig, and there is a complication that breeders have to consider: it is recognized that if a guinea pig (especially one of the longhaired breeds) is extensively exhibited, this will negatively affect its breeding

Cream and buff guinea pigs. A pair of guinea pigs that are to be mated should be introduced on neutral ground. This can help to reduce the chance of a fight.

Left: Guinea pig litters average two to four in size.

A breeding program requires an investment of time and money if it is to be successful. If you don't have the time and resources for such an endeavor, don't breed your guinea pigs.

This guinea pig is not accustomed to being held. Guinea pigs that do not like to be handled are not good prospects as exhibition animals.

potential. You therefore have three basic strategies from which you can choose:

1. To select the very best youngsters and retain them for breeding. You then exhibit the second-best from your litters.
2. To exhibit a youngster but withdraw it from your show team while it is still young enough to retain its willingness to be bred.
3. To exhibit your best youngsters from alternative litters so that you are retaining the very best for both needs. This is easier for the owner of a large stud to do, especially when the general standard of his stock has reached a high level of consistency.

The final advice to would-be exhibitors is that they

must devote considerable time to handling their show guinea pigs. There is little point in trying to exhibit a guinea pig that will not take up a show position. It will be impossible to judge an individual that is clearly terrified of all that is going on around it!

Visit a number of shows before you commit to this area of the hobby. You will be better able to decide whether it really appeals to you and whether you have sufficient dedicated enthusiasm to be successful. You will really enjoy your time at the show, learning much about these fascinating pets, and meeting many interesting people.

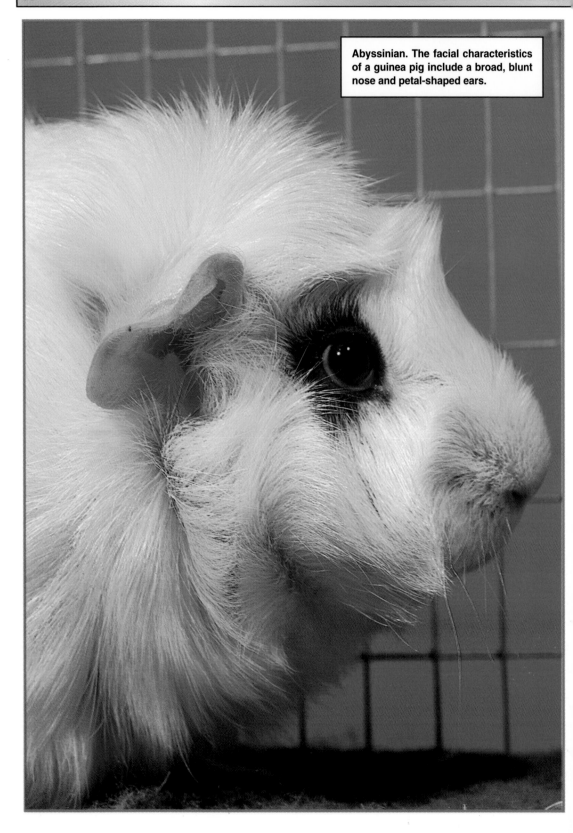

Abyssinian. The facial characteristics of a guinea pig include a broad, blunt nose and petal-shaped ears.

HEALTH PROBLEMS

Probably the most quoted, and most disregarded advice given to beginners with respect to their pet's health care is that of cleanliness. But it really is the most important area of husbandry, along with nutrition and stress avoidance, in minimizing the risk of having to deal with problems.

ROUTINE HYGIENE

This subject covers everything from daily and weekly cleaning of the cage, to correct storage of foods and personal hygiene. For breeders, it also means keeping the stockroom and its adjacent areas spotlessly clean and free of any form of garbage that could house pathogens or their hosts, such as mice or rats.

Cracked and chipped food/water vessels should be replaced as soon as damage is noticed.

It is important that you always wash your hands before handling your pet, and especially if:
1. You have visited a friend who owns guinea pigs or other rodent pets.
2. You have been gardening without wearing rubber gloves. Many bacteria live in garden soil.
3. You have just handled a guinea pig that is, or is suspected to be, ill.
4. You have visited a guinea pig show or another show where various livestock are on display. It is easy to transport pathogens

into your home via your hands or clothing. Breeders are advised to wear clean nylon coats when attending routine chores in their stockroom.

QUARANTINE

If you already keep guinea pigs or add to your first pet, it is wise to quarantine additional individuals for at least 14 days to ensure that

Bathe your pet only occasionally: overbathing can cause dry skin.

they are not incubating any disease or problem, even if their source maintained excellent husbandry standards. This advice is very important to breeders.

The quarantine area should be as far away from other pets as possible. During this transitional period, you can carefully observe the new arrival, gradually making any deemed changes in its diet.

Have your vet do a fecal analysis to see if there are signs of excess worm eggs.

STRESS

This condition, which is very difficult to pinpoint, is a major precursor of problems and illnesses in pets. This is especially so in guinea pigs, which are by nature very shy and nervous little animals.

Stress can affect your

guinea pig in three ways. It can induce syndromes, meaning abnormal behavior patterns, can reduce the performance of the immune system, and can reduce the pet's ability to correctly utilize vitamin C.

The degree of stress is thought to be directly linked to the importance of elements in the guinea pig's environment that are needed for its general well being, but that are being denied to the animal. On this basis, any of the following may induce stress: lack of space, incorrect diet, unclean housing that forces the pet to live in squalor, sudden and loud noises, excessive disturbance, lack of regular handling, changes in its environment, excessive heat or cold, bullying by other guinea pigs or pets, and lack of a retreat in its cage.

Not all guinea pigs will be affected to the same degree. To complicate matters, some problems, such as syndromes, may not be a direct result of stress. They could be caused by the lack of a particular mineral or vitamin, or by some other metabolic problem that only your vet can determine.

However, it is generally accepted with guinea pigs that stress is a very significant factor in many diseases, conditions, and problems, including those related to breeding and birthing.

RECOGNIZING ILL HEALTH

There are two ways in which you can recognize ill health in your guinea pig. It will display clinical signs or changes in its pattern of behavior.

Clinical signs: Discharge of liquid from the eyes or nostrils; dull, cloudy looking eyes; any form of swellings, sores, or abrasions; diarrhea, constipation, blood-streaked urine; dry looking hair and skin; flaking of the skin; bald areas; visual signs of parasites or their presence (eggs, scurf, black specks); sneezing; coughing; labored

It's a good idea to give your guinea pig a daily once-over. The sooner a problem is discovered, the sooner treatment can be effected.

and noisy breathing; vomiting; slobbering; and any form of limping or the inability to move as normal.

Behavioral signs: Lack of interest in food or water; excessive drinking; huddling in a corner when normally active; general lethargy; loss of weight; twitching; reluctance to being handled coupled with obvious pain

when lifted; and excessive scratching. Indeed, any pattern of behavior that you have never noticed before should be viewed with suspicion.

Sometimes behavioral signs will be the only visual indicators of a problem. For this reason, it is important that you spend time observing your pet when it is eating. You can establish whether it is a greedy or dainty eater, what foods are its favorites, and how often and how much it drinks.

DEALING WITH HEALTH PROBLEMS

Once you suspect that your guinea pig is not well, do not wait for matters to get worse before you react. Contact your vet, who will be able to tell you, based on the information that you supply, whether you need to visit the clinic as soon as possible, or to wait another twelve hours to see if the problem clears up. It may be that it is of a minor sort, such as a temporary tummy upset, a chill, or their like.

As a general precaution, if you suspect an illness, it is wise to move the pet's cage to an area where it is a little warmer, and quiet. If diarrhea is evident, withhold moist foods pending advice from the vet, but maintain

A guinea pig and a rabbit can be kept to-gether, provided that the rabbit is not one of the larger sized breeds. A rabbit has strong hind legs and an accidental kick could injure a guinea pig.

the water supply. A breeder should remove any animal that is suspected of ill health away from the rest of the stock as soon as is possible.

If the clinical signs seem serious, gather some fecal samples in a plastic container and place them in the refrigerator (never the freezer). Your vet may want them for microscopic examination.

If a guinea pig is clearly ill, you will need to completely clean its cage and discard bedding and any twigs or other soft items.

Hygiene now becomes especially important, so be sure to wash your hands before and after handling the pet. Disposable surgical gloves are a useful item to have at this time.

LEAVE DIAGNOSIS TO YOUR VET

If you cherish your guinea pig, you will not attempt to diagnose and treat a health problem. The clinical signs

of ill health may be caused by a multitude of pathogens that may be affecting the respiratory or digestive systems. They may be problems of the urogenital system, or of organs such as the liver or heart.

Your vet will need to conduct tests to establish causal organisms, and only when this is done can a suitable treatment be determined. Listening to the well-intended, but uninformed, advice of so-called "expert" friends is a very dangerous way to proceed.

Guinea pigs (and hamsters) react very badly to certain antibiotics. Antibiotics such as penicillin, streptomycin, tylosin, and lincomycin are invariably fatal to these particular animals. They kill the gram-positive and beneficial gut flora, allowing the gram-negative organisms to proliferate. Death usually follows within four to nine days.

Maintain the proper feeding regimen and provide good-quality food.

Indiscriminate use of modern drugs will also result in harmful bacteria developing resistance to the drug. For every sensible reason, you should rely totally on the diagnosis and treatment coming only from your vet. The dosage and duration of treatment is also a matter of importance with guinea pigs.

PARASITES

A guinea pig can become infested with either and/or both ectoparasites and endoparasites in the form of lice, mites, and various worms, as well as by fungus, whereby the condition is called ringworm.

Lice and mites, apart from causing alopecia (hair loss), may be the means by which more noxious pathogens enter the body via the small lesions that they create. They can be seen by using a

In general, guinea pigs are hardy animals, but they can fall victim to a number of illnesses. Good husbandry will go a long way in helping to keep your guinea pig healthy.

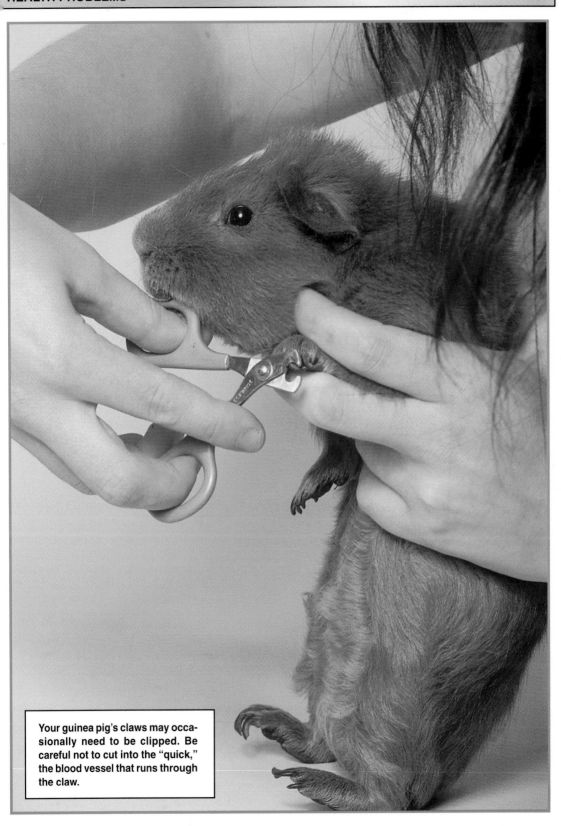

Your guinea pig's claws may occasionally need to be clipped. Be careful not to cut into the "quick," the blood vessel that runs through the claw.

good magnifying glass. They will appear as tiny creatures that move slowly, and their eggs appear as clusters of specks. However, hair loss alone can have other causes, such as that seen in stressed sows during gestation and the postpartum period. Control of ectoparasites can be achieved with dichlorvos strips suspended above the cage or in the breeding room for 24 to 48 hours; repeat the procedure at two-week intervals for 2 to 3 treatments. Ivermectin given orally under veterinary advice is an alternative treatment.

Internal parasites such as worms can be identified via flotation methods and egg counts by your vet. Treatment is with ivermectin or other vet-recommended drugs. Complete eradication of internal parasites is often difficult because the eggs are readily airborne. Fortunately, low levels of infestation are unlikely to cause any major problems. General hygiene is the best preventive strategy in the control of parasites.

Ringworm is transmissible to humans and other animals. It is characterized by bald, reddened areas of skin that are flaky and encrusted. They may be on the face or body. The inclusion of griseofulvin (2.5mg/100g body weight) in the diet is beneficial. Vet-recommended creams or other treatment should be effective, coupled with high standards of hygiene.

When a guinea pig has diarrhea, especially during warm weather, flies can become a major hazard. They lay their eggs in organic

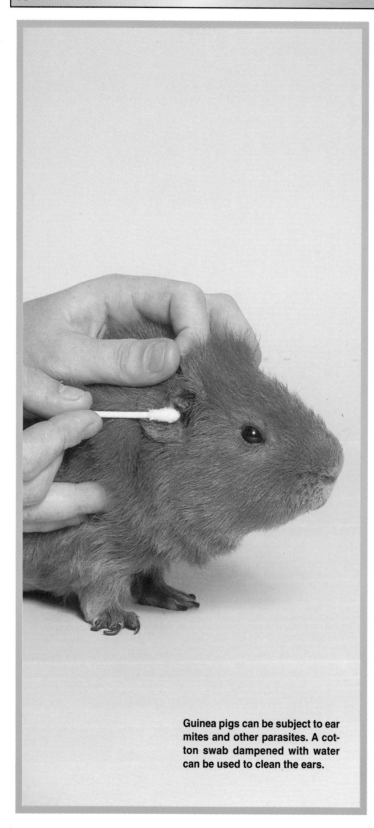

Guinea pigs can be subject to ear mites and other parasites. A cotton swab dampened with water can be used to clean the ears.

insecticides as they can be toxic to your pet.

CHECK YOUR GUINEA PIG ON A REGULAR BASIS

Diseases and other harmful conditions in guinea pigs can invariably be avoided by correct husbandry techniques. However, you can strengthen your general care regimen by regular physical examinations of your guinea pig. This should be done every time you handle it. By doing so, you will be able to spot problems before they get out of hand. Include inspection of the teeth and toenails to see that they are not getting too long. Nails are easily trimmed with guillotine-type clippers. Be sure to trim only the tips to avoid the risk of cutting into the blood vessel, or "quick." This is especially important with dark-colored nails, in which the blood vessel is not readily seen.

matter, such as fecal matter clinging to the skin of the guinea pig's rear end. The larvae of these flies (maggots) burrow into the skin, releasing toxins in the process.

Via the lesions created, bacteria can become established; and the guinea pig may rapidly suffer a major disease. Eradication of maggots is by their individual removal, using forceps; treatment will be required to protect the damaged skin. Longhaired breeds are likely to be more susceptible to this sort of parasitic problem than shorthaired breeds.

During very fly-active periods, it will be helpful to cover your pet's cage with a fine mesh, which will greatly reduce the potential for these pests to gain access to the guinea pig and its food and bedding. Old-fashioned sticky fly strips suspended above the cage are another safe yet effective control. Avoid the use of aerosol

Above: A black guinea pig enjoying some sunshine and fresh air. Some black guinea pigs may have a brownish hue to their coats. *Below:* This guinea pig's cage is badly in need of a cleaning. Dirty accommodations greatly increase your pet's chances of getting sick.

BREEDS & COLOR VARIETIES

When selecting a guinea pig, your first consideration should always be its coat type. Generally, the average pet owner is not advised to obtain the longhaired breeds— the Peruvian or the Silky (Sheltie in UK). Considerable time must be devoted to the grooming and general care of these breeds; otherwise, their flowing coat can rapidly

advice cannot be overstressed.

THE BREEDS

There are presently about eleven breeds recognized by the various ruling associations of the US and the UK. Each association has its own way of classifying the breeds, and color names may vary on either side of the Atlantic. However, the basis of the

similar to the normal coat but has a satin-like sheen to it.

SMOOTH-COATED GUINEA PIGS

Smooth-coated guinea pigs are numerically the most popular and the easiest to care for from a practical viewpoint. Their coat is short and sleek. Their temperament is arguably the most steady of the many breeds. This does not imply that the other breeds are not good, but that the smooth-coated guinea pig is the oldest of the breeds and has been bred to a very high standard of excellence as far as temperament is concerned. Its type is also superb in top show stock, often being used to improve the conformation in other breeds.

The Crested is the same as the smooth coated but sports a rosette of hair on the crown. In the US, the crest is white, the body color being any accepted color except those that feature white in them. In the UK, the crest is usually the same color as the body and is also seen in patterned varieties.

The rosette in a quality specimen should be a complete circle radiating evenly from a central point. Its position on the crown is important in an exhibition individual.

Tricolor and blue point Himalayan guinea pigs. The smooth-coated guinea pigs are the easiest to care for.

deteriorate into an unsightly mass of tangles.

In such a state, the coat readily becomes a haven for lice, mites, and fleas, all of which will create subsequent problems. The tangles alone will be the source of mats that present serious difficulties. These problems will make life intolerable for longhaired breeds. The need to heed this

breeds is international, so for our purposes we can divide the breeds into the following groups: 1.) smooth coated: American (Self in the UK), Crested; 2.) non-smooth coated: Abyssinian, Teddy; 3.) longhaired: Peruvian, Silkie.

In each of these groups except for the Crested, there are normal and satin-coated alternatives. The satin is

ABYSSINIAN

This breed displays a harsh coat that forms rosettes over the body and head. As with the Crested, the rosettes should radiate from a pinpoint

Pink-eyed cream guinea pig.

center. There should be at least ten rosettes in a good example: one on each shoulder; one on each side of the saddle (the mid-section of the body); one on each hip; and two on each side of the rump. A high ridge of hair should form wherever two rosettes meet. The rosettes account for 65 of the 100 points allocated for judging this breed, so they are a very important feature. In pet examples, the ideal specimen described is not usually apparent, with the rosettes often being incomplete, and areas of flat hair visible.

TEDDY

This is one of the newer breeds and one that will become increasingly popular as the coat is steadily improved by breeders.

The mutation that creates this breed, which appeared at about the same time in both England and Canada, is called rex. Its effect is to dramatically reduce the length of the guard hairs of a normal coat. The result is that the woolly underfur develops as a wavy, or crinkled, coat that stands away from the body. The coat length should be 1.9cm ($^3/_4$ in.), either rough or plush to the touch, both being acceptable. There should be no flat areas in the coat. The whiskers are also crinkled.

The rex mutation is seen at its best in the rabbit. Someday the guinea pig may sport a comparable deep, resilient, and plush coat that will make it a truly magnificent breed.

PERUVIAN

This longhaired breed's coat may grow to over 51cm (20 in.) and requires daily grooming. The coat length has steadily increased from that seen in specimens during the 19th century. Unlike the normal flow of an animal's hair—from head to rump—the hair of this breed radiates from rump rosettes, so that it flows forward over the head, shoulders, saddle, and rump in a circular manner.

The coat should be dense and soft, having a very high sheen to it in the satin variety. Longhaired breeds may suffer from many problems related to their hair, one of which is the ingestion of hair. The

A pair of young Teddies. In some countries, this breed is known as the rex.

result can be hairball block-
ages in the digestive tract. Hay
is an essential aid in prevent-
ing this potentially dangerous
condition.

A pet Peruvian can have its
coat trimmed to a more suitable length, thereby making
management infinitely more
easy and at the same time
making life more pleasant for
the pet. Be sure to trim the
area over the eyes: this will
help make the pet less nervous. It is quite unnatural for
animals to sport coats of the
length seen in guinea pig
breeds; so if you decide to own
a longhaired specimen, be
very sure you are committed
to its grooming needs.

SILKIE (SHELTIE)

The Silkie's hair flows
naturally from head to rump,
so it is more typical of
longhaired variants as seen in
dogs, cats, and some other
animals.

The breed is of relatively
recent origin; but in its short
history, it has already developed a coat length comparable
to that of the Peruvian. Unlike
the Peruvian's hair, the hair
on this breed does not fall all
over the guinea pig's face, but
flows over the neck like a
mane. Its management needs
are exactly the same as those
for the Peruvian.

GUINEA PIG COLORS AND PATTERNS

Considering the wide range
of colors and coat patterns
that are seen in guinea pigs,
there is certain to be one that
will appeal to you. Indeed,
there are so many that you
may have difficulty making
your choice. All of the guinea
pig breeds are available in all
of the colors discussed here.

Above: White crested and golden and white. These are pet-quality guinea pigs. *Below:* Dalmatian youngster. This color variety is named after the dog breed of the same name. Dalmatian guinea pigs have grown in popularity in recent years.

The exception to this comment is in regard to white cresteds, which have some restrictions placed on them for exhibition purposes in the US, and possibly in other countries.

The following details the present color and pattern range. However, new colors are gradually being developed by new mutations that spontaneously appear and by recombinations of existing mutations. The colors are arranged into four groups, which we will discuss in

chocolate, beige, buff, cream, lilac, red, red-eyed orange (self golden in the UK), and white.

In a quality individual, the color should be as even as possible over the entire guinea pig. Other than in the black or white, a color may display a range of intensities from light to dark (e.g., light or dark cream). These shades may be given their own names by some breeders, though your

not detract from your pet's qualities as a companion.

SOLID COLORS

A solid– color guinea pig has a color pattern that is uniform over its entire body, including the belly (thus agouti is not a member of the solid color group). A solid color is created by the intermixing of white with one or two different colors.

In the solid roan, the head may be either agouti or of a self color, with the solid pattern

White and tri-color Abyssinians. The ideal body conformation of this breed is to be rounded, with plenty of depth to the shoulders and hindquarters. The coat is to be dense and of sufficient length to form deep rosettes and ridges.

the following order: self, solid, agouti, and marked.

SELF COLORS

A self color is that in which the entire guinea pig is of the same color. There must be no ticking in the coat. In the UK, the term *self* also designates a show group that is restricted to the smooth-coated (shorthaired) breeds. All others are in the non-self group, which would therefore include the self Abyssinians and the longhaired breeds.

Self colors are black, blue,

ruling association is the ultimate authority for the correct names and their description. But even in black or white guinea pigs, there will be differences in the quality of the color. A good black should be deep, like that of a crow or coal. A white should be chinapottery white. Many blacks will display a brown hue to the coat; some whites will show yellow.

In pet-quality self varieties, you will no doubt find some foreign hairs, meaning those of a different color. They will

commencing at shoulder level.

The brindle is a mixture of red and black, but some areas may display a small group of the same colored hairs. However, these should not form any sort of pattern. Other solid colors are golden, silver, and dilute. These solids should be as in the agouti, but the color extends over the entire abdomen.

AGOUTI

This is the original color pattern of the wild guinea pig and is named for the South

Peruvian guinea pig. The coat of the Peruvian is very dense, with a soft, silky texture.

Above: Lilac sow. In self-colored guinea pigs, the density of color can vary somewhat from specimen to specimen. *Below:* American, or cream self, guinea pig. The body of this breed is medium in length with broad shoulders. The coat is short and silky.

American rodent. Agouti is seen in many animals, especially rodents, because it forms a natural camouflage against bushes, rocks, sand, and light filtering through foliage.

The pattern is created by each hair shaft being banded in light and dark colors. The natural lie of the coat results in a ticked appearance. The abdomen is a uniform white, or it may be colored, depending on the variety; it must be free of any ticking. Present agouti color varieties are:

Golden—This color should display a rich chestnut hue created by the banding of red and black over a blue-black base. The belly is a deep red.

Silver—The appearance is that of silver, which is created by black ticking over white. The belly is white.

Dilute—There are potentially fourteen variations of dilute. The hair tips may be cream, orange, red, or white. The base color is beige, black, chocolate, or lilac. Various combinations of these colors give 16 variations. However, red tipped over black, and white tipped over black base are not acceptable because they represent golden or silver agouti, which have their own standard. The terms cinnamon, lemon, lilac, and argente agouti are used by some breeders to describe forms of the dilute agouti.

MARKED COLOR PATTERNS

A marked pattern is a variety in which a color is broken up to form an orderly pattern, usually on a white base. This group contains many beautiful guinea pigs, including those that might not win show awards due to technical faults in their pattern but which are exquisite and quite unique. The following are the most popular marked varieties:

Broken—This variety sports patches of color, of which a minimum of two must be at least the size of a 50-cent piece. Ideally, the patches should have clearly defined edges and be uniformly placed on the body. The pattern can be seen in a multitude of forms, each slightly different from the other.

Dutch—Named for the pattern that is so popular in rabbits, the Dutch is always an attractive variety. The cheeks are colored, the rest of the head and forepart of the body white, with the remainder of the body a color that matches that of the cheeks.

This color begins just behind the front legs and should form a complete circle around the body. The line of demarcation between white and color should be as clean and straight as possible.

Any self or agouti color is acceptable on the colored portion of the body. Breeding quality Dutch guinea pigs is difficult because many will be mismarked.

Dalmatian—A relatively modern variety, the Dalmatian is a spotted pattern. The spots should be as numerous and well defined as possible. Obtaining consistency in this pattern is all but impossible because it is not directly under breeder control. There is a strong element of chance involved in producing well-marked individuals.

Himalayan—This pattern is seen in many popular pets. The body should be as white as possible with the points

Above: Young tri-color guinea pig. *Below:* Red Abyssinian sow and litter. The youngsters are almost ready to be weaned.

(ears, nose, and feet) being black or chocolate. Obtaining really black points is difficult because the color is thermosensitive. This means that as the temperature rises, the points' color gets lighter. Black points are therefore usually dark chocolate, with the chocolate variety being a lighter shade.

In theory, it is possible to have any color on the points. In due course, you will no doubt see new colors appearing and gaining recognition.

Tortoiseshell—This pattern is created by regular checkerboard patches of red and black. In an exhibition animal, the colors patches must be of equal size. It is a difficult variety to breed to a high standard of marking, and consequently it is not highly popular.

In contrast, the tortoiseshell and white variety is quite well known. In it, the three colors of red, black, and white should ideally form patches alternating with each other on each side of the body. The patches meet along the back and down the abdomen in a straight line. This variety is difficult to produce to a high standard, so even show individuals rarely attain perfection. But the color pattern, even on poorly

A nicely marked bi-color Abyssinian.

marked guinea pigs, is still very attractive.

Bicolored pattern—This pattern is the same as for tortie, except that the red is replaced by white. A tricolored equivalent to the torties and white is also available. The harlequin has the colors of black (or chocolate), yellow, and brindled. If the yellow of the harlequin is replaced by a combination of white and blue roaning, it is called a magpie.

DEVELOPING BREEDS AND VARIETIES

Among the breeds and varieties being developed at this time, and which may in due course become established, are the following. The eventual name popularly applied to them may not be the same as that used here.

The Ridgeback has a ridge of hair running down the length of its back. It is a variation on the Abyssinian. The crested

mutation has been combined with the Peruvian coat to create the crested, or coronet, longhaired guinea pig. Long hair has also been combined with rex to produce the longhaired Teddy (Rex).

Not all combinations of hair type will prove to be winners. In some instances, the genes can work in an antagonistic manner. For example, the hair of the Teddy, when combined with long hair, produces

Above: This Dutch-marked guinea pig is about to enjoy a treat. The Dutch color pattern can also be seen in a number of other animals. It is very popular. *Below:* American crested. In an ideal specimen of this breed, the crest will rise and radiate evenly all around. It will be clean, bright, and even.

individuals that are inferior to either parental variety. Only time will tell if any beneficial results will justify crossings utilizing mutations that would not at first seem logical.

While there may be a limit to the potential of coat types that can be produced, the same is not true of colors and their patterns. The saffron is a creamy lemon color that has become popular. The sable is another color that is being carefully refined.

In the realm of patterns, there is always potential for new varieties that may be banded or striped in the manner of the tabby pattern seen in cats. A final cautionary word is appropriate to those planning to breed roans and whites. The dominant white mutation (Wh) involved produces no negative effect when in single (heterozygous) dose but creates the condition known as microphthalmia when in double (homozygous) dose. The result is individuals with very tiny pink eyes.

When breeding roans (and Dalmatians), it is wise to mate a roan with its self base color. This means that a blue roan would be mated to a self black. A strawberry roan would be mated to a self red. This avoids the condition just discussed. The resulting offspring carrying the white gene will always have it in the heterozygous state ($Whwh$).

This white gene is not the same mutation that produces the white in other patterns such as the Dutch. It underscores the need for any potential breeder to gain some working knowledge of the science of genetics if he wishes to avoid matings that might produce negative features in some of the offspring.